dissolutions ov refraction

A.A.F.

Published by Arthur A. Filgueiras
Paperback ISBN 979-8-218-84085-3
Hardcover ISBN 979-8-218-84086-0

Cover and sigil design by A.A.F.

dissolutions ov refraction is the second collection of poems by A.A.F.
and continues the descent begun in *the ephemeral nature ov* (Liber I-III).

Illustration Credits:

Image on page 12 is from *Dogme et Rituel de la Haute Magie* by Éliphas Lévi (1856).
Image on page 24 and 36 are from
A Collection of Emblemes, Ancient and Moderne by George Wither (1635).

All images are in the Public Domain, sourced from the Internet Archive.

these poems are a testament to my refraction(s).

contents

VIII

...if you gaze long into an abyss, the abyss also gazes into you.

— Friedrich Nietzsche,
Beyond Good and Evil, Aphorism 146

per benedictionen YHWH.

maledictus HWHY...adumbratur.

Liber IV:

the Split

?!

drifting
into a shadow

ov another,

shapeless.

leviathan
ov endless faces

none
to choose.

my soul(s)
hidden in

their own veil.

exhausted
by mirrors

with no *reflection(s).*

i saw its mask.
almost

it(s) saw me.
almost

both seen
almost

so you said
so you said.

so i said
so (we) said.

who is speaking?

two bodies
faced *away*.

(n)either together,
(n)or alone.

presence
ov no one.

no one
is present.

presence
is no one.

who. am. I?
who. are. you?

we. are. us.

together / apart.

Liber V:

the Coil

soul searching
leaves only

a soul searching.

purpose
finds only
dead ends

end
begins.

suffocates.

begins
end.

devouring
the other

excreting
another
to *re-devour*

layers
ov flesh
layered
on flesh

lies
without *core.*

withered skin

ov a snake's
missed shed

still withering

flesh
urinated
to expose

my *selve(s)*.

menstruated
flesh
dissolved.

another one
discarded

voiceless speech
vomiting words
fills the air

where are you now?
i'm home

there was never a home.

where are you now?
not home.

where are you now?

Liber VI:

the Still

stillness night
cricket chirps
to its *shadow*

vast horizons
it stands.

directionless

kind eyes
empty

the *smile*
ov a knife.

open space

indefinitely sealed.

sharpened edges

thoughts
within thoughts
ov thoughts.

fully thoughtless.

in solace.

a vulture
patiently *waits*.

drowning
in silent voices.

surface(s)
without reach.

we kiss
speaking tongues
tasteless
we kiss

in *numbness*
i am comforted.

self-embraced.

i am the *me*
within the (i).

a nobody
with
no body.

tonight
i died.

cigarette
still lit.

!?

maledictus.

…adumbratur.

dissolutions ov refraction

A.A.F.

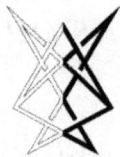

all words were solely human written

www.ingramcontent.com/pod-product-compliance
Lightning Source LLC
La Vergne TN
LVHW041204080426
835511LV00006B/737